KS.

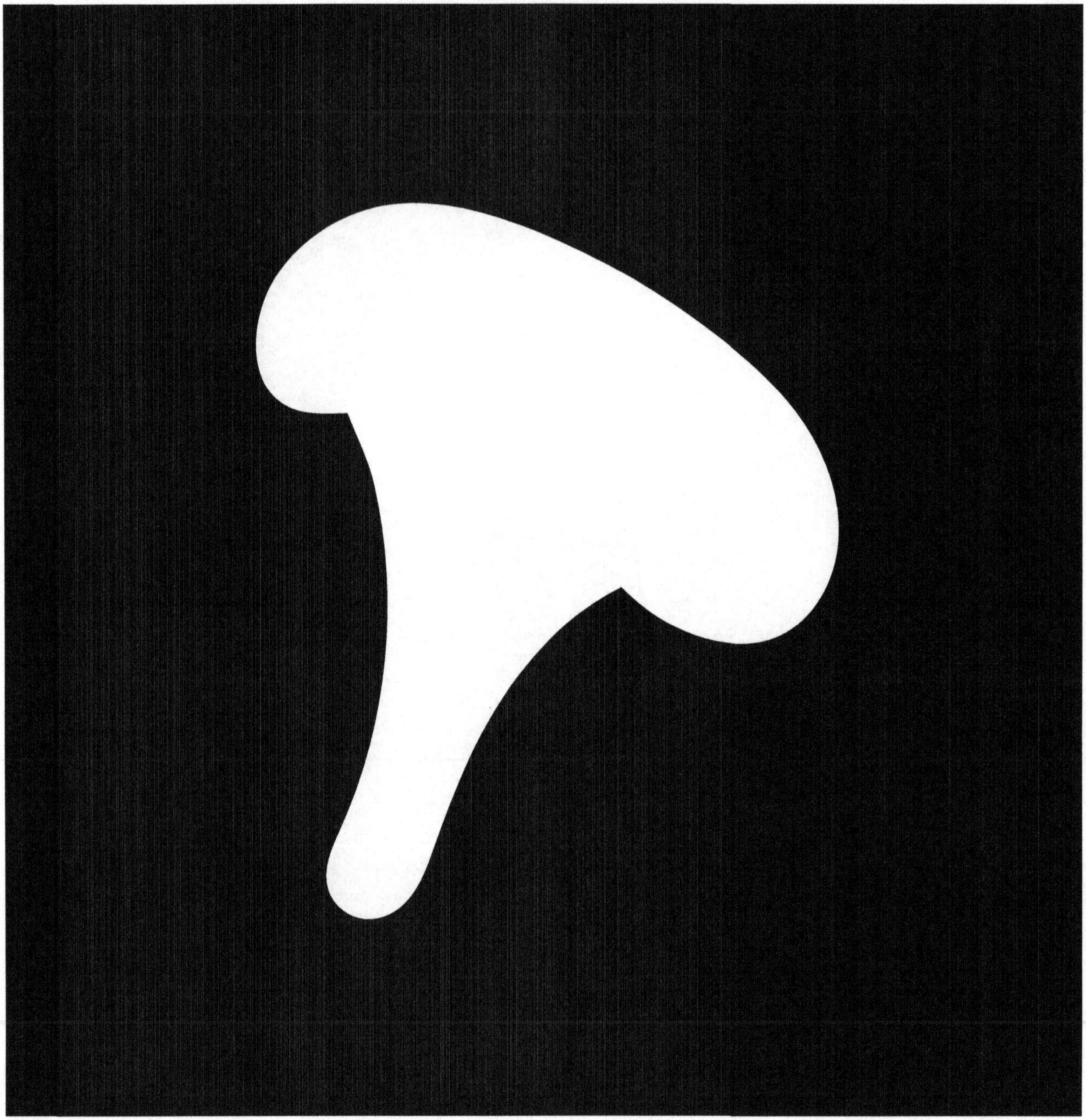

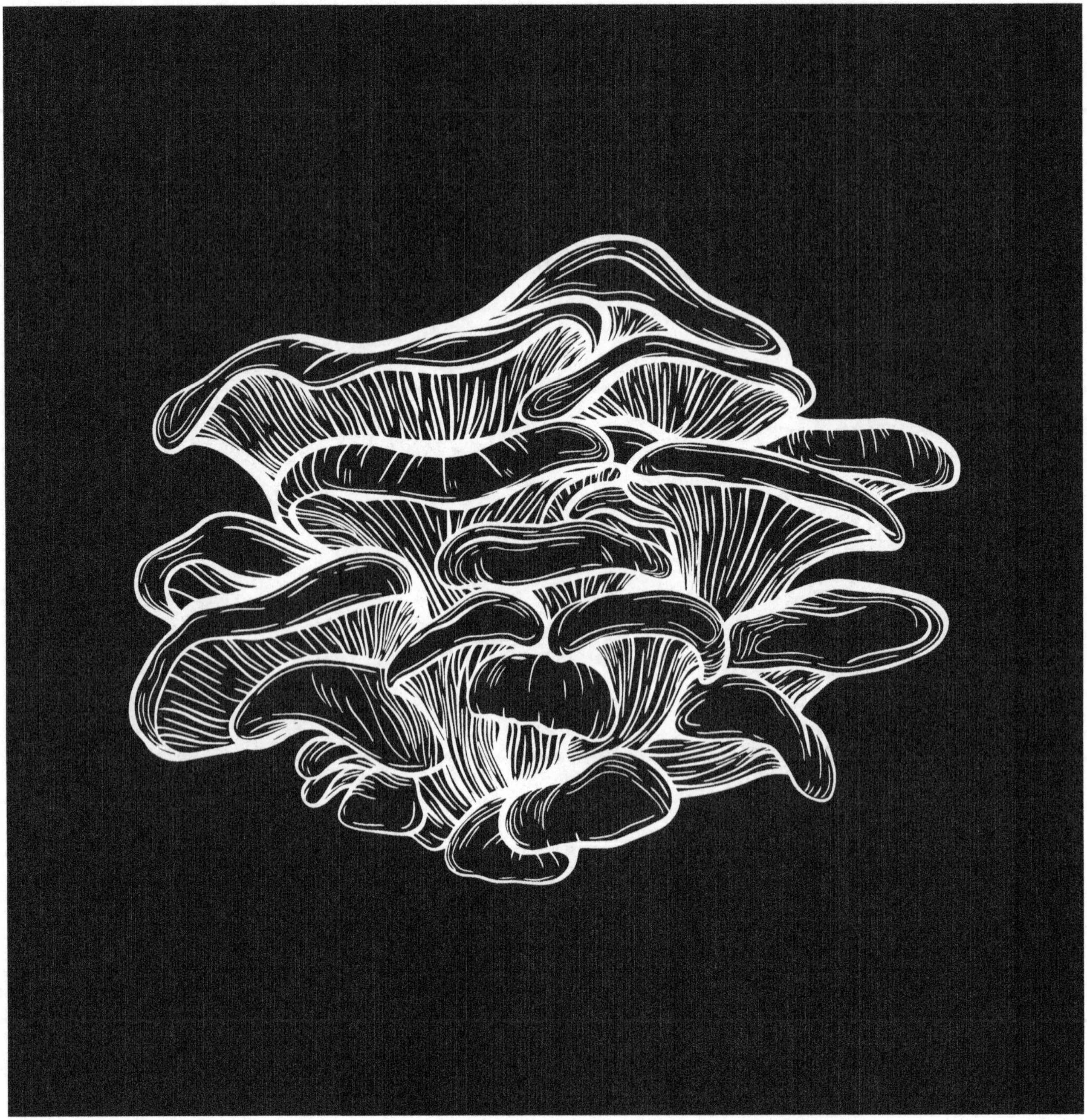

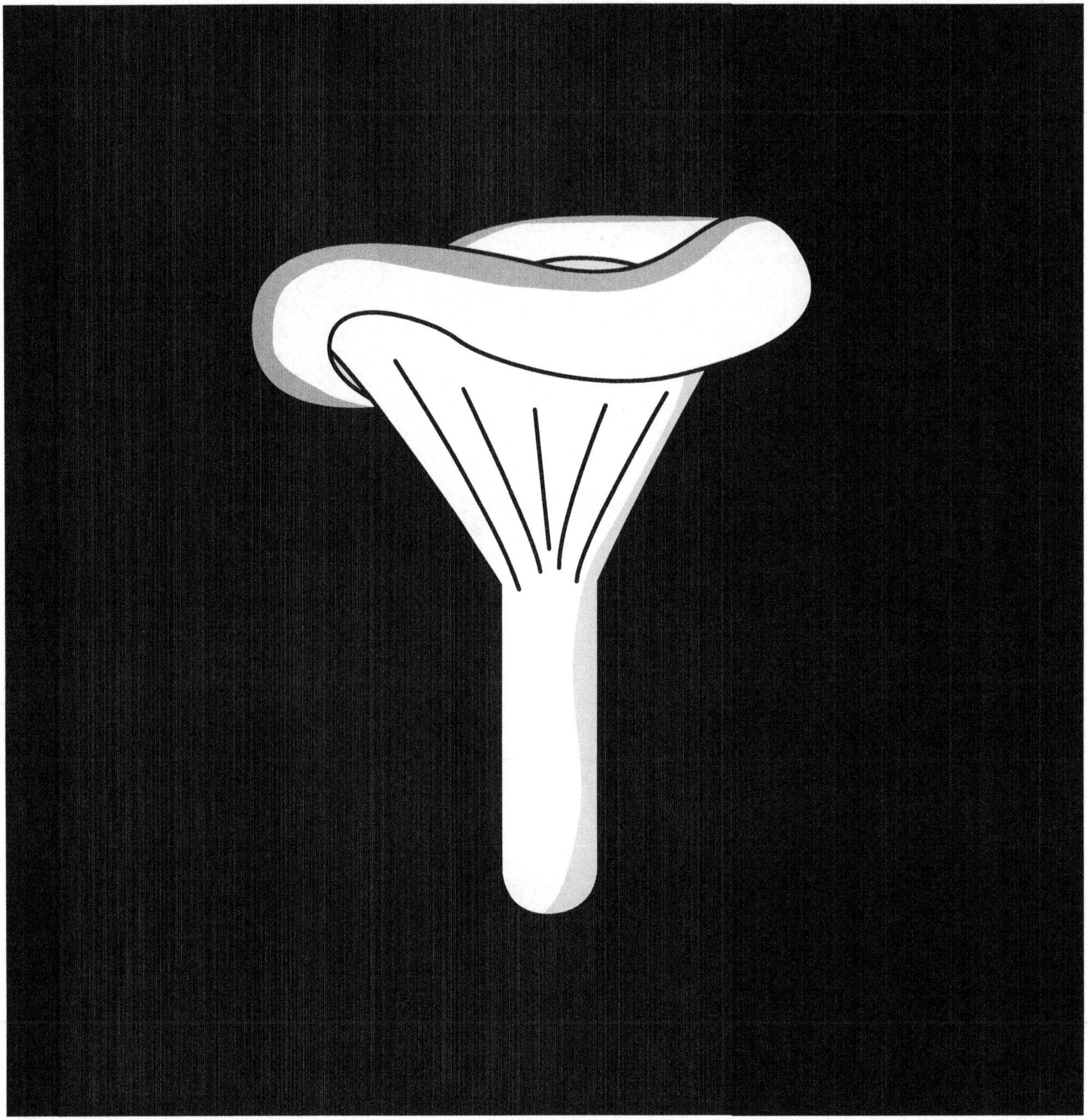

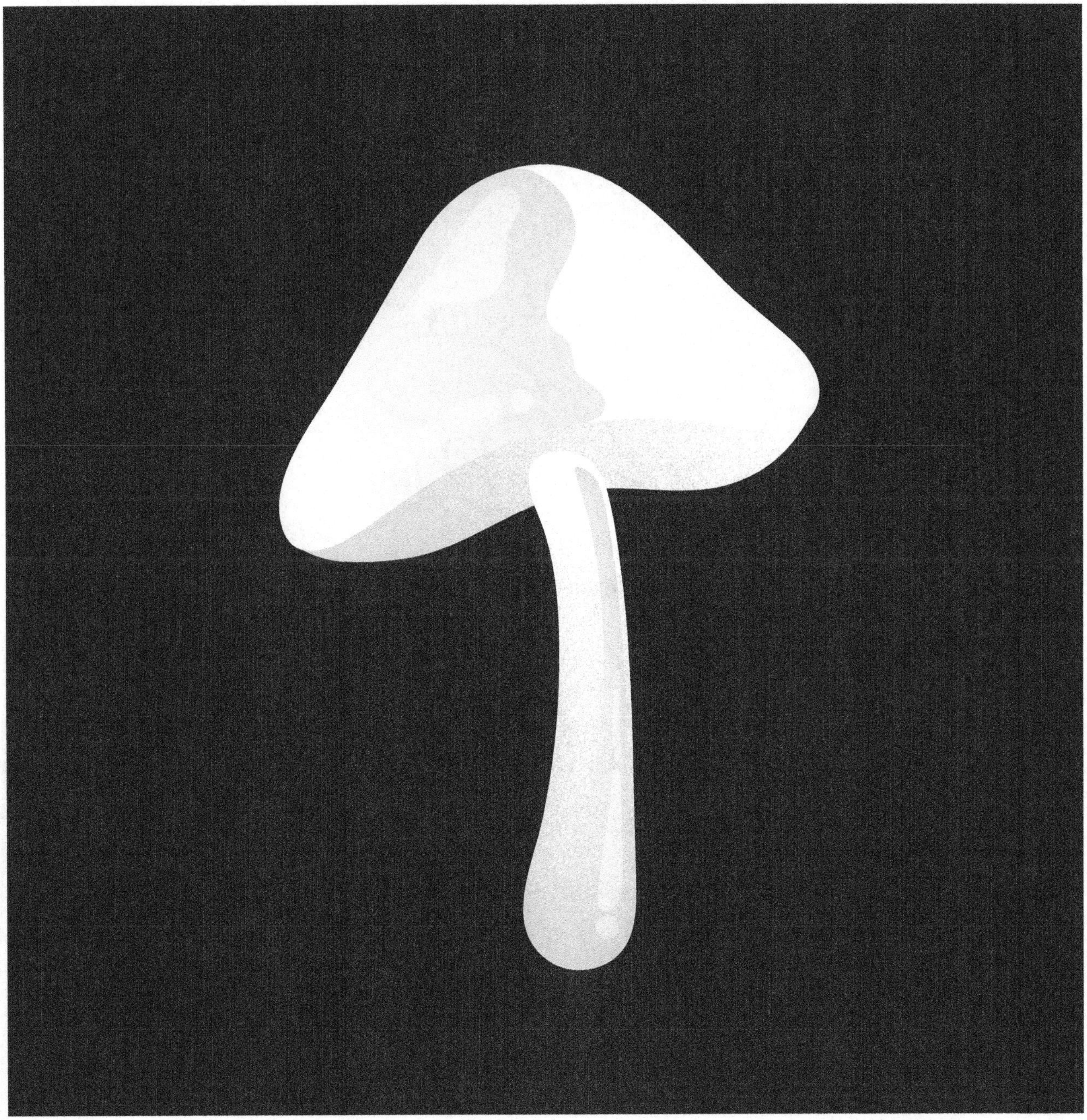

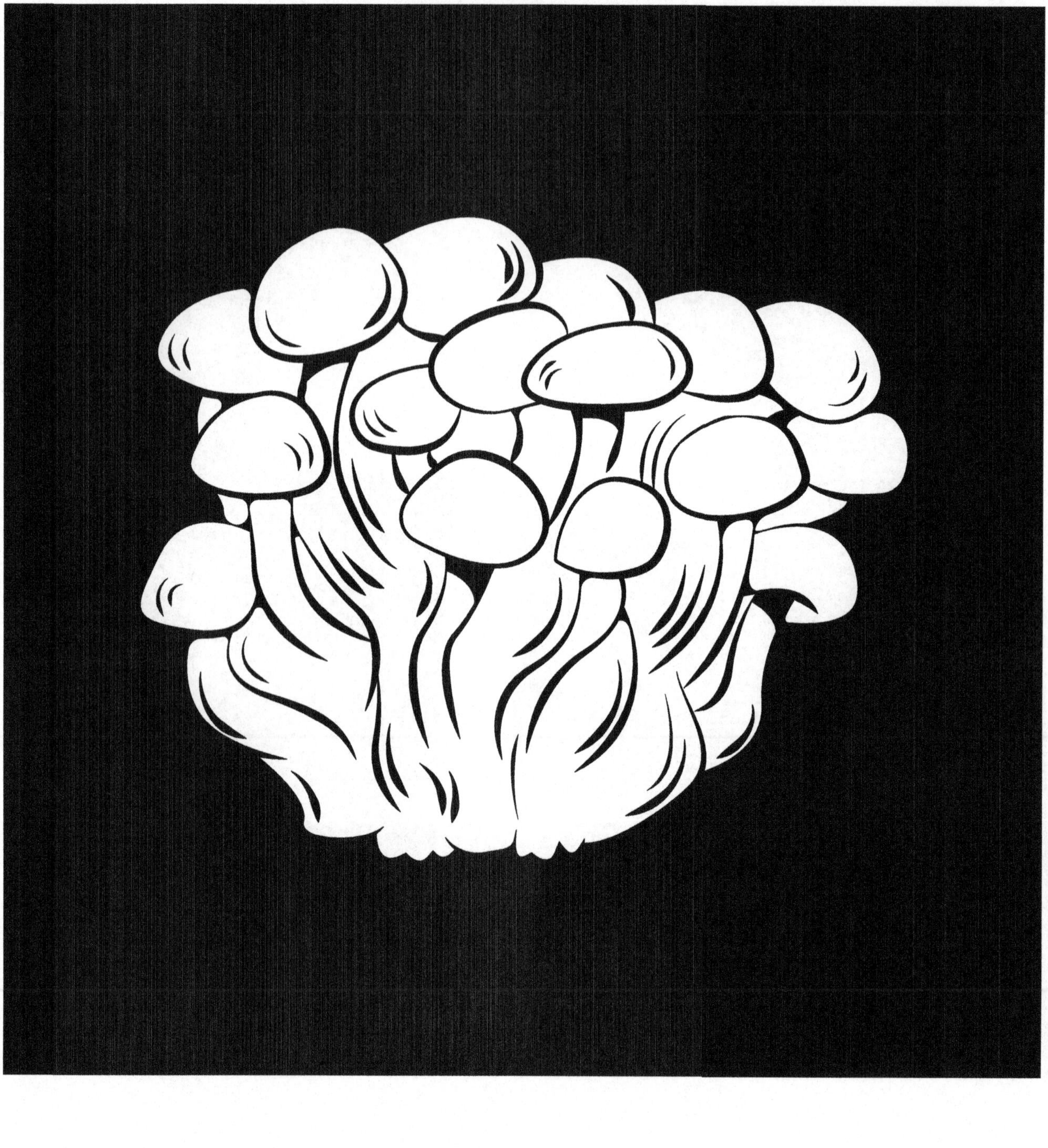

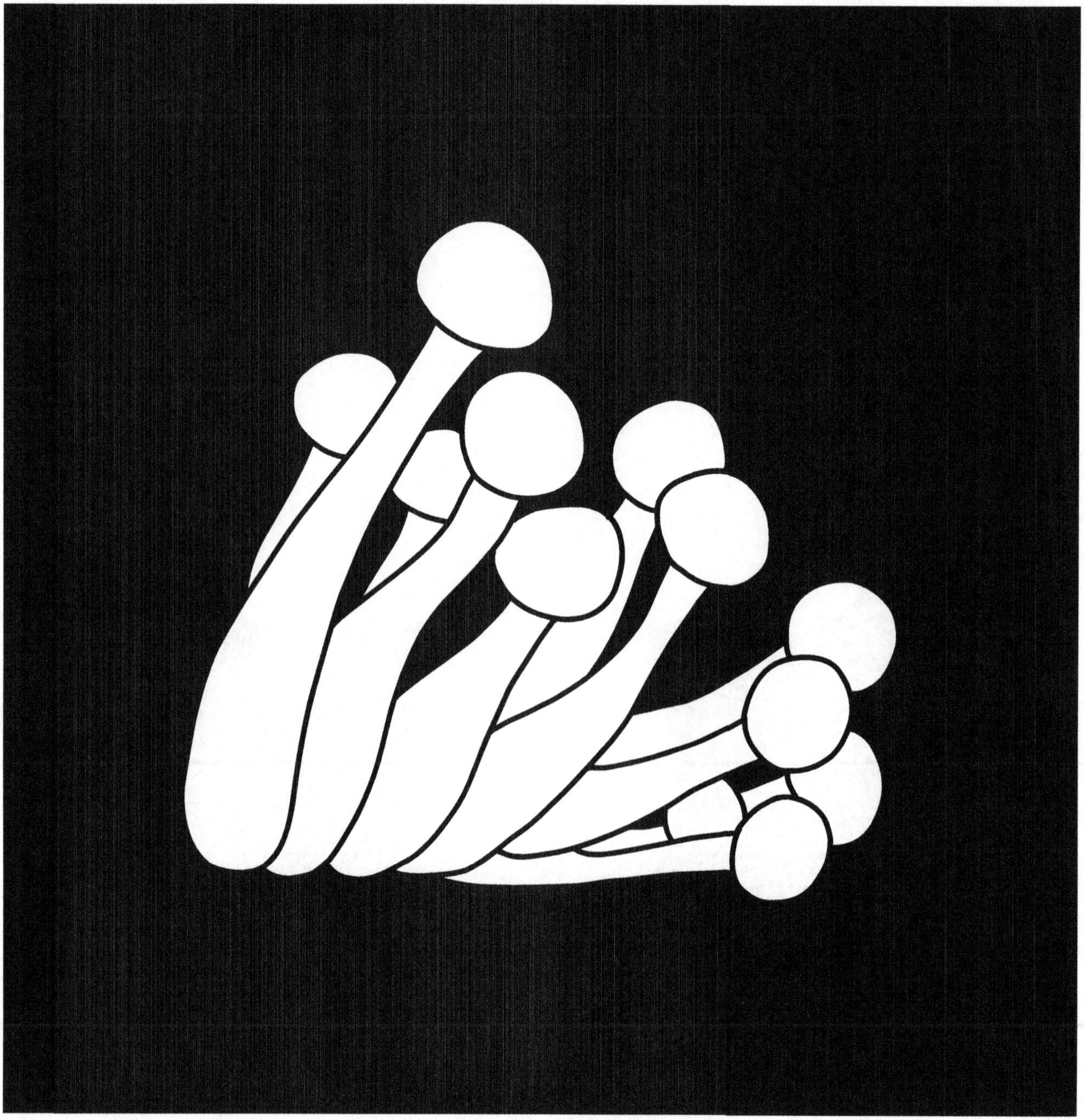

Printed in Great Britain
by Amazon

44232822R00020